Learning Is Fun!

KATHY ROSS C·R·A·F·T·S

TRIANGLES, RECTANGLES, CIRCLES, AND SQUARES!

by Kathy Ross

Illustrated by Jan Barger

The Millbrook Press
Brookfield, Connecticut

To Emily and Adam

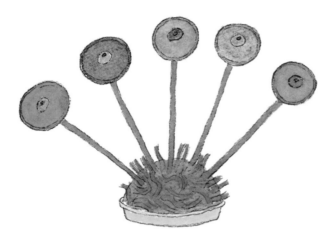

Library of Congress Cataloging-in-Publication Data
Ross, Kathy (Katharine Reynolds), 1948-
Kathy Ross crafts triangles, rectangles, circles, and squares / Kathy Ross ;
illustrated by Jan Barger.
p. cm. — (Learning is fun)
Summary: Provides step-by-step instructions for twenty easy crafts intended to teach
about four basic shapes: circles, squares, triangles, and rectangles.
ISBN 0-7613-2104-7 (lib. bdg.) — ISBN 0-7613-1696-5 (pbk.)
1. Handicraft—Juvenile literature. 2. Geometry - Juvenile literature.
[1. Handicraft. 2. Shape] I. Barger, Jan, 1948- ill. II. Title. III. Learning is fun!
(Brookfield, Conn.)
TT160. R714235 2002   745.5—dc21   2001044770

Published by:
The Millbrook Press, Inc.
2 Old New Milford Road
Brookfield, Connecticut 06804
www.millbrookpress.com

Printed in the United States of America
lib: 5 4 3 2 1
pbk: 5 4 3 2 1

Table of Contents

KATHY ROSS
C•R•A•F•T•S

TRIANGLES, RECTANGLES, CIRCLES, AND SQUARES!

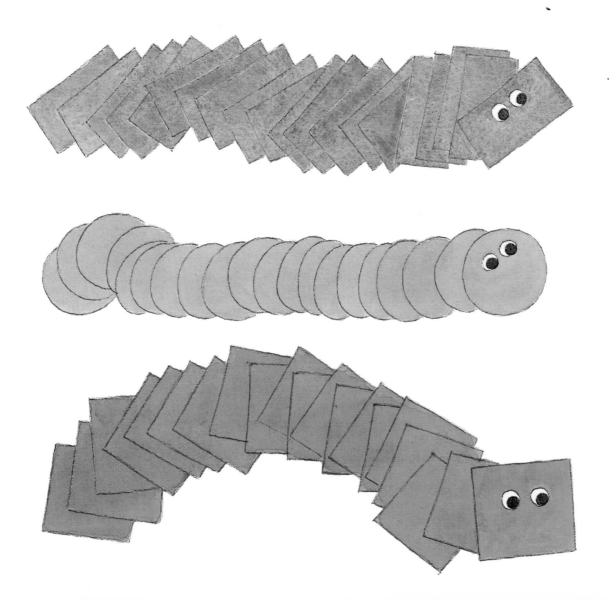

Introduction

Circle, triangle, rectangle, and square are not only the first shapes that children are taught to recognize in preschool, but they are also my favorite crafting shapes. My young students have always had a lot of fun with them.

Children love making the circle friend puppet from a discarded compact disc or a square friend from a newspaper crossword puzzle. They eagerly watch the grass growing to form a "hairy squary." And clipping triangle corners from old envelopes to make bookmarks gives them the satisfaction of making useful items from shapes.

In addition to helping your children have a good time while learning basic shapes, these craft projects will also enhance shape recognition and awareness of the recurring presence of shapes in the world.

All that little learners will need are scissors, glue, some simple household items, and their own sense of fun to create shape crafts with pizzazz and personality.

Kathy Ross

Circle Friend

Make a round puppet from a discarded compact disc.

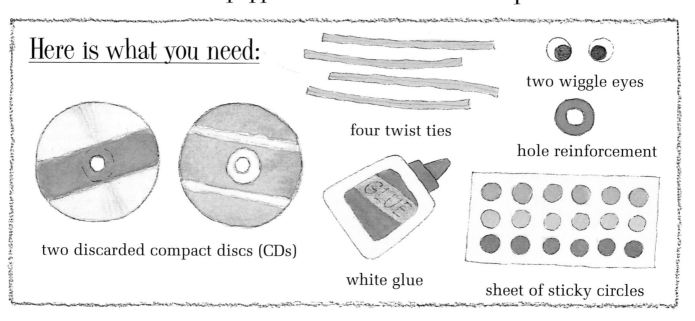

Here is what you need:

four twist ties

two wiggle eyes

hole reinforcement

two discarded compact discs (CDs)

white glue

sheet of sticky circles

Here is what you do:

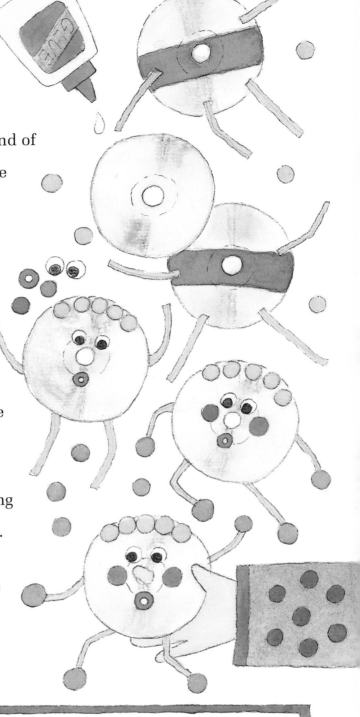

1. Cover the print side of one CD with glue.

2. Put the end of a twist tie in the glue on each side of the CD to stick out to form arms. Put the end of two more twist ties in the glue at the bottom of the CD to hang down to form the legs of the puppet.

3. Place the second CD, print side down, over the first, to become the front of the puppet.

4. Glue the two wiggle eyes to the front CD just above the hole. Stick the hole reinforcement below the hole in the CD for the mouth. Use some of the sticker circles to make the hair and cheeks.

5. Make hands and feet for the puppet by sticking two circles together over the end of each twist tie.

6. Stick your own finger through the hole in the CD puppet to give the circle friend a funny nose.

CDs are fun to use to make rubbings of **circles**. Just put the CD under a sheet of paper and rub over it with the side of a peeled crayon to make a **circle** shape appear on the paper. Make lots of **circles** in different colors.

Rubber Band Circles Picture

Here is an idea for making a picture out of **circles**.

Here is what you need:

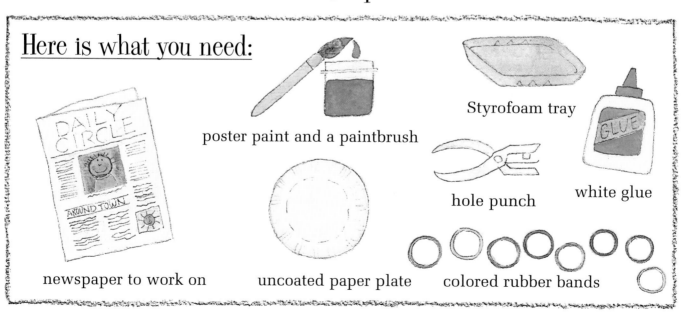

poster paint and a paintbrush

Styrofoam tray

hole punch

white glue

newspaper to work on

uncoated paper plate

colored rubber bands

Here is what you do:

1. Paint the eating side of the paper plate a bright color or leave it white.

2. Arrange the rubber bands as circle shapes to make a picture or design on the paper plate.

3. When you are satisfied with your rubber-band picture, pour some glue on the Styrofoam tray. Dip each rubber band in the glue and stick it back in place on the plate.

4. Punch a hole at the top edge of the plate. Thread one end of a rubber band through the hole, then thread the other end through the first end and pull it tight to make a hanger for the picture.

You might want to keep a collection of rubber bands loose in a box to use to make circle pictures and designs. Line the lid of the box with a sheet of construction paper and use it as a frame for your pictures. When you are done, just put the rubber bands back in the box, ready to play with on another day.

Circle Flowers Stabile

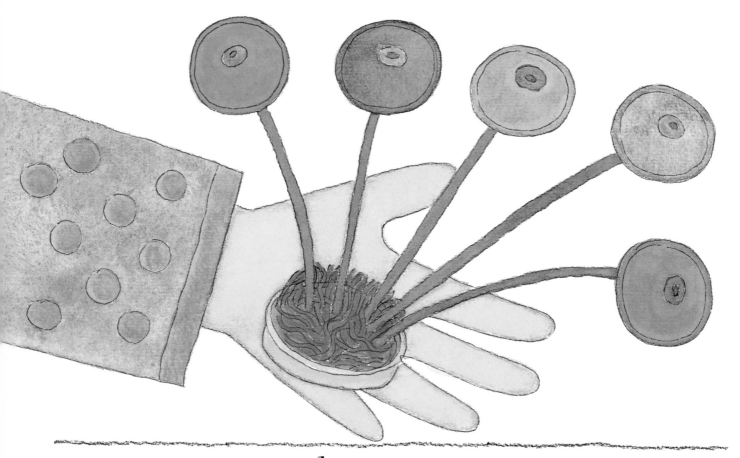

Make these pretty **circle** flowers to keep or to give as a gift.

Here is what you need:

five colored plastic milk-jug caps

white glue

green yarn

small jar (such as baby food) lid

scissors

five 6-inch (15-cm) green pipe cleaners

five craft beads

2-inch (5-cm) Styrofoam ball

Here is what you do:

1. Ask a grown-up to cut the Styrofoam ball in half with a knife.

2. Glue a half of the Styrofoam ball into the lid to make the base for the stabile.

3. Poke a tiny hole in the center of each milk-jug cap.

4. Poke one end of each pipe cleaner through the hole on the top side of each cap to make the flowers.

5. Cover the pipe-cleaner end at the center of each flower with glue, then cover it with a craft bead to make the flower centers.

6. Stick the stem of each flower into the Styrofoam base. Arrange them on the base so that they are balanced and will stand without tipping over.

7. Cover the Styrofoam around the flower stems with glue.

8. Cover the gluey Styrofoam with small pieces of green yarn to look like grass.

Make a pretty circle flower picture by dipping the end of an empty thread spool in paint and printing circles on a piece of paper. Print lots of different color circles, then use a marker to add stems, leaves, and other details to the picture. Spool flowers look nice on the front of homemade greeting cards.

13

Circle Shake Game

Give these **circles** a shake to get them into place.

Here is what you need:

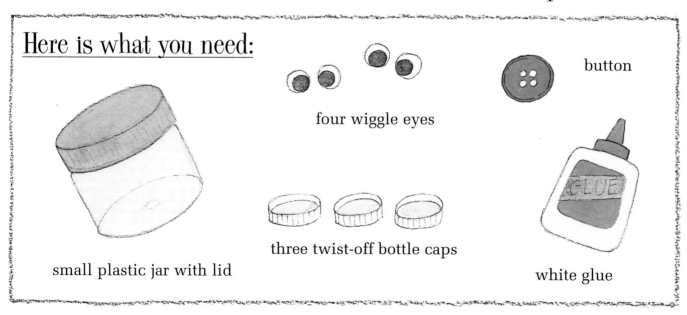

four wiggle eyes

button

three twist-off bottle caps

small plastic jar with lid

white glue

Here is what you do:

1. Glue the three bottle caps inside the lid of the jar, top side down.

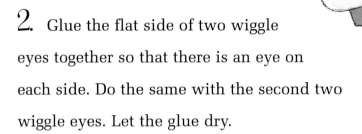

2. Glue the flat side of two wiggle eyes together so that there is an eye on each side. Do the same with the second two wiggle eyes. Let the glue dry.

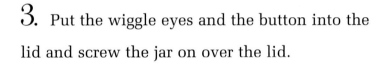

3. Put the wiggle eyes and the button into the lid and screw the jar on over the lid.

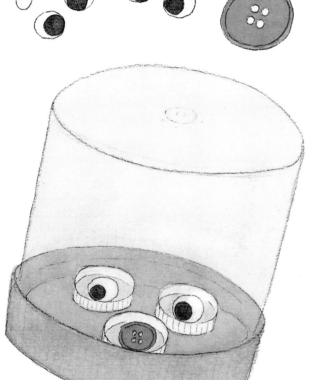

4. Try to shake the button and the two eyes each into a different cap to look like a face.

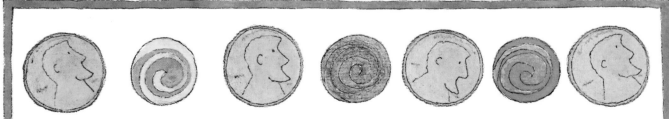

What other round things might you use in your puzzle? How about some pennies?

Circle Buttons Fun

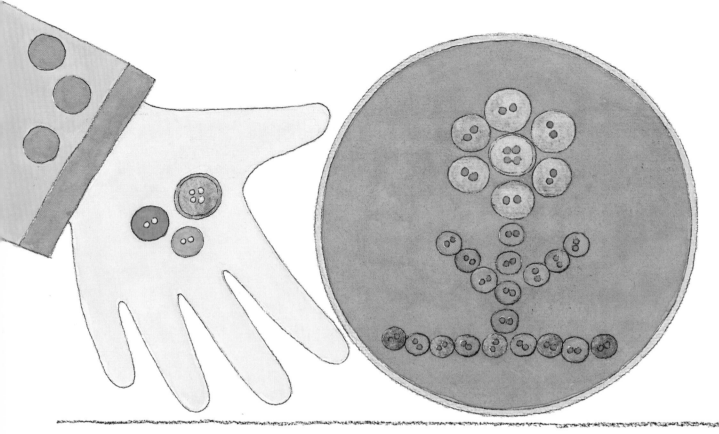

Collect colorful round buttons to make endless pictures and designs from **circles**.

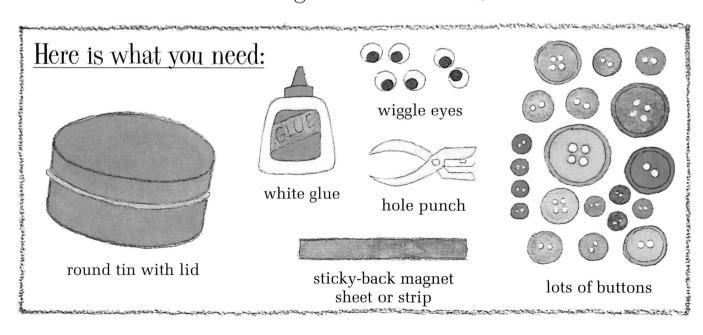

Here is what you need:

wiggle eyes

white glue

hole punch

round tin with lid

sticky-back magnet
sheet or strip

lots of buttons

Here is what you do:

1. Arrange some buttons on the lid of the tin in a pretty design or picture. Glue the buttons to the lid to decorate it.

2. Punch a hole from the sticky-back magnet for each button and each wiggle eye.

3. Stick a magnet dot on one side of each button and each wiggle eye.

4. Store the buttons and eyes in the tin, and when you want to play, just stick them to the inside lid of the tin to make button pictures and designs.

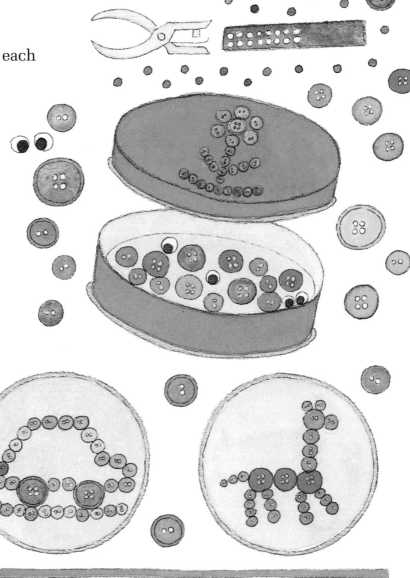

Want to make a whole page of **circles** fast? Paint a sheet of bubble wrap and use it to print **circles** on a sheet of construction paper. Fun!

17

Happy Triangle

Make yourself a bouncy **triangle** buddy!

Here is what you need:

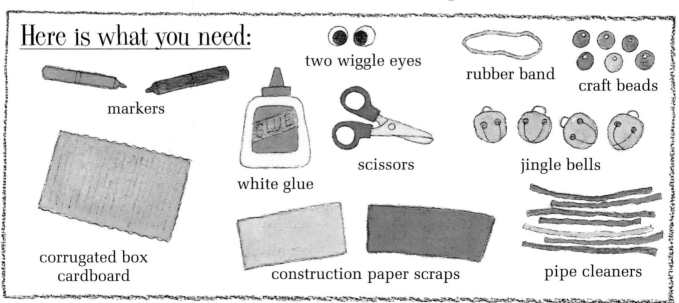

two wiggle eyes

rubber band

craft beads

markers

white glue

scissors

jingle bells

corrugated box cardboard

construction paper scraps

pipe cleaners

Here is what you do:

1. Cut a triangle shape from the cardboard.

2. Turn the triangle so that the ridges in the cardboard run up and down.

3. Cut triangle-shaped eyes and a nose from the construction paper scraps. Glue them to the front of the triangle. Glue a wiggle eye to the center of each triangle eye. Use a marker to give the triangle friend a smile.

4. Insert the end of a piece of pipe cleaner dipped in glue between the cardboard on each side of the triangle to make arms. Insert two more pipe-cleaner pieces dipped in glue in the holes between the cardboard at the bottom of the triangle to make legs.

5. Cut a construction paper triangle to glue at the end of each pipe-cleaner arm and leg to make triangle hands and feet.

6. Wrap pieces of pipe cleaner around your finger to make spirals. Thread craft beads and a jingle bell on each spiral to decorate. Thread an end of each spiral into the top of the triangle to give it a very festive look.

7. Cut the rubber band. Glue one end to the top of the back of the triangle. When the glue is dry you can bounce the triangle on the rubber band to hear it jingle.

You might want to slip some other things into the holes in the corrugated cardboard to decorate the **triangle**. How about some feathers or some artificial flowers?

19

Triangle Birds

Turn a **triangle** shape into a bird.

Here is what you need:

pipe cleaner

marker

scissors

craft feather

construction paper in three colors

masking tape

white glue

Here is what you do:

1. Cut a triangle from construction paper with all of the sides the same length.

2. Fold the points of the triangle in on each side for the wings.

3. Bend the top point down without creasing the fold and secure the point with a small piece of tape. This will be the head of the bird.

4. Cut a small triangle beak from construction paper and glue it over the taped point of the head. Cut two eyes from construction paper and glue them on the head above the beak.

5. Glue the craft feather to the top of the head.

6. Glue the ends of two pieces of pipe cleaner to the bottom back of the bird so that they hang down to form legs.

7. Cut two small triangles from construction paper to glue on the end of each leg for feet.

8. Cut two small triangles from construction paper for baby birds. Fold the top point of each triangle down for the head. Use a marker to draw a beak and eyes on each bird.

9. Fold the points on each side of each triangle in to form wings for the baby birds.

10. Glue a baby bird under each wing of the large triangle bird.

Folding **triangles** to make animals is fun! You might want to try folding the side points up to make the head of a cat or down to make the head of a dog. What else can you make?

Triangle Handbell

Make a bell that is shaped like a **triangle**.

Here is what you need:

12-inch (30-cm) pipe cleaner

scissors

sticker stars

jingle bell

ruler

small cereal or food box

aluminum foil

cellophane tape

Here is what you do:

1. Cut a 2- to 2 1/2-inch (5- to 6-cm) corner from the side of the box. The triangle corner will be the base for the bell.

2. Cover the corner base with aluminum foil. Use cellophane tape to secure any loose edges.

3. Poke a tiny hole through the top of the triangle.

4. Fold the pipe cleaner in half and thread the two ends down through the hole in the top of the triangle. Thread a jingle bell onto one end of the pipe cleaner, then twist the two ends together to secure the bell.

5. Pull the top part of the pipe cleaner into a loop so that the bell hangs down inside the triangle.

6. Decorate the outside of the bell with sticker stars.

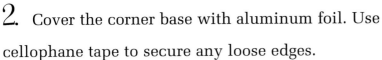

Triangle box corners are fun to make things with. Try turning a corner over and adding a handle to make a little basket to hang on a doorknob or pushpin.

Triangle Page Markers

These **triangle**-shaped bookmarks make a nice surprise to tuck inside a note or letter.

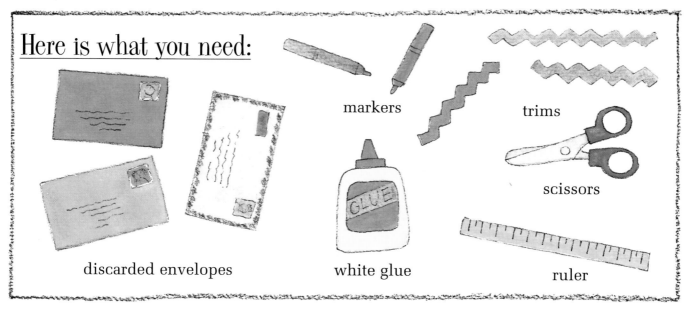

Here is what you need:

markers

trims

scissors

discarded envelopes

white glue

ruler

Here is what you do:

1. For each marker you are making, cut a corner from the bottom of an envelope that is about 4 inches (10 cm) across the bottom cut side of the triangle.

2. Decorate both sides of the triangle using the markers and gluing on trims.

3. To use the triangle page marker, slide the open end of the triangle over the corner of the page to be marked.

Cut some corners from envelopes and turn them into **triangle** finger puppets. You can make an entire family of **triangle** friends in no time!

25

Triangle Lapel Pin

Wear a **triangle** on your shirt collar!

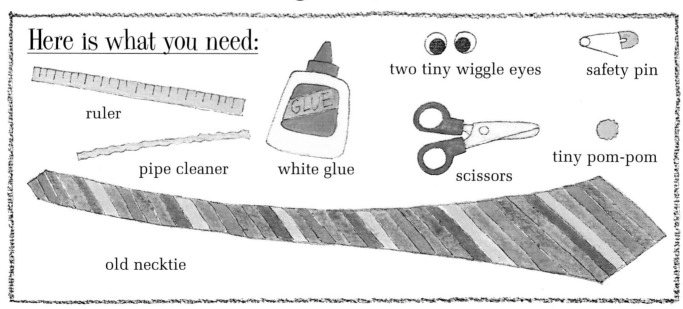

Here is what you need:

ruler

pipe cleaner

white glue

two tiny wiggle eyes

scissors

safety pin

tiny pom-pom

old necktie

Here is what you do:

1. Cut a triangle that is 3 inches (8 cm) across the bottom from the tip of the necktie.

2. Cut a 6-inch (15-cm) piece of pipe cleaner. Fold the pipe cleaner in half to make legs for the triangle. Bend the ends forward to form feet.

3. Cut a 4-inch (10-cm) piece of pipe cleaner for the arms. Wrap the fold of the legs around the center of the arms to attach them to the legs.

4. Cut a tiny slit in the fabric about halfway down each side of the triangle.

5. Poke an arm through each hole from the inside of the tie triangle so that an arm sticks out on each side of the triangle and the legs hang down from the bottom.

6. Fold the ends of the arms to make hands.

7. Glue the two wiggle eyes to the top of the triangle and the pom-pom nose under them to make a face.

8. Attach the safety pin to the back of the triangle so you can wear it as a pin.

> For some silly **triangle** fun cut a long **triangle** shape from cardboard. Use markers, cut paper, and collage materials to decorate the **triangle** like a pizza slice with your favorite toppings on it.

Mr. Rectangle

This puppet is made of **rectangles** only.

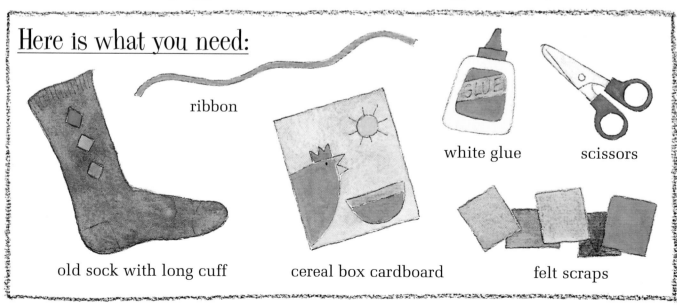

Here is what you need:

ribbon

white glue

scissors

old sock with long cuff

cereal box cardboard

felt scraps

Here is what you do:

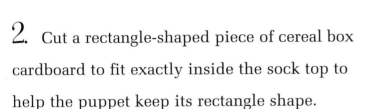

1. Cut the top part of the sock off the foot to use as the body of the puppet.

2. Cut a rectangle-shaped piece of cereal box cardboard to fit exactly inside the sock top to help the puppet keep its rectangle shape.

3. Cut rectangle-shaped eyes and eyebrows from the felt scraps for the puppet. Make him a rectangle nose and mouth. Glue the face pieces to the front of the top part of the sock puppet.

4. Cut strips of ribbon for hair for the puppet. Glue the ends of the ribbon to the top of the cardboard insert so that it sticks up from the top of the puppet.

5. Glue the top of the sock to the front and back of the cardboard insert to secure it.

Take **Mr. Rectangle** on a hunt for **rectangles** around your house.

Smoking Rectangle Chimney

A chimney is shaped like a **rectangle**.

Here is what you need:

wooden ice-cream spoon   penny wrapper   ruler   cotton ball

paper   white glue   scissors   markers

Here is what you do:

1. Trim the penny wrapper to just under 3 inches (8 cm) for the rectangle chimney. Use the markers to add details to the chimney.

2. Cut a 3 1/2-inch (9-cm) square of paper. Fold the paper in half to make a roof for the house. Use the markers to add details to the roof.

3. Glue a puff of cotton "smoke" to the bowl end of the wooden spoon. When the glue has dried, slip the spoon up through the penny wrap chimney so that by pushing on the handle of the spoon the cotton "smoke" comes up out of the chimney.

4. Cut a slit in the top center fold of the roof. Slide the bottom part of the chimney into the slit in the top of the roof. Glue the back of the bottom part of the chimney to the back inside of the roof to secure it.

5. Cut a 3-inch (8-cm) square of paper to make the house. Add details to the house with the markers. Glue the top part of the house to the bottom of the inside of the front of the roof.

Use rectangle-shaped money wrappers to make finger puppets. Use markers or glue on collage materials to create different faces for each puppet.

Rectangle Pussycat Puppet

Turn a discarded padded envelope into
a **rectangle**-shaped puppet.

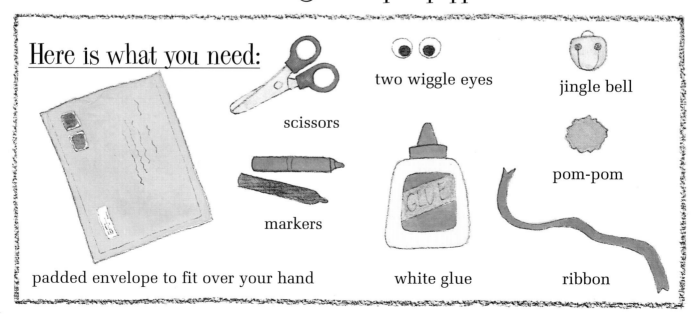

Here is what you need:

two wiggle eyes

jingle bell

scissors

pom-pom

markers

white glue

ribbon

padded envelope to fit over your hand

Here is what you do:

1. Turn the padded envelope so that the opening is at the bottom. Fold the top two corners of the envelope forward at an angle to form the ears of the cat. Add a triangle-shaped inner ear using a marker.

2. Glue the two wiggle eyes to the envelope below the ears. Glue the pom-pom below the eyes for a nose. Add details to the face, such as a mouth and whiskers, using a marker.

3. Cut a strip of ribbon for a collar for the cat. Glue the ribbon across the middle section of the envelope, below the mouth. Glue a bow made from the same ribbon to the collar. Glue the end of the jingle bell to the center of the bow.

Instead of making a puppet you might want to stuff the rectangle pussycat with Styrofoam packing bits or crumpled newspaper. Glue the bottom shut and secure it with clamp clothespins until the glue is dry.

Rectangle Jewelry

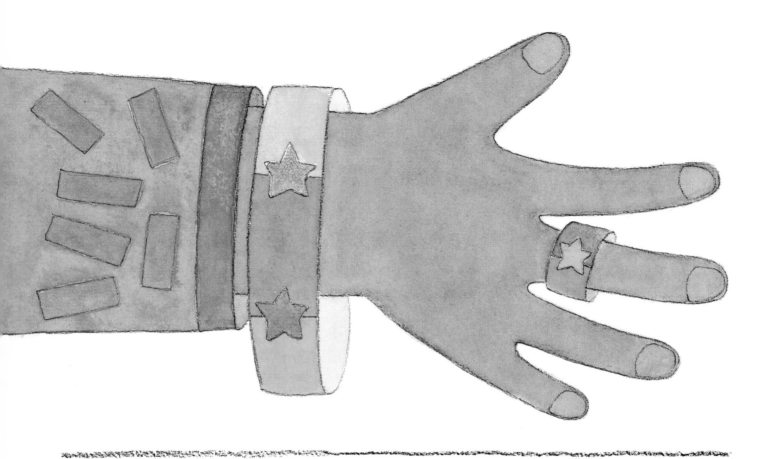

Here is an idea for **rectangles** to wear.

<u>Here is what you need:</u>

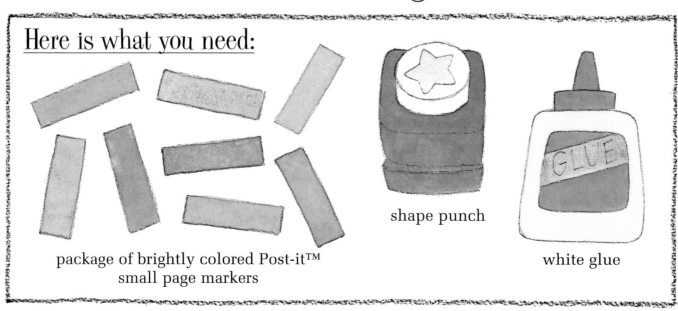

package of brightly colored Post-it™
small page markers

shape punch

white glue

Here is what you do:

1. Stick enough colored page markers together to make a long rectangle bracelet that will fit your wrist.

2. Carefully unstick each strip and re-stick it with glue. Glue the two ends together to make a bracelet that will slip over your hand.

3. Use the shape punch to punch shapes from different colored page markers.

4. Decorate the bracelet by gluing on the punched shapes.

5. Use this same idea to make a rectangle ring.

Stick a line of colorful page markers on a sheet of construction paper. Use markers to add details to the picture to make it look like a train.

Rectangle Collage

Create a very fancy **rectangle** to display.

Here is what you need:

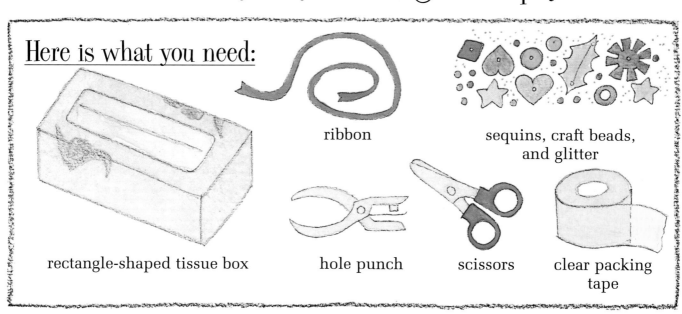

rectangle-shaped tissue box

ribbon

sequins, craft beads, and glitter

hole punch

scissors

clear packing tape

Here is what you do:

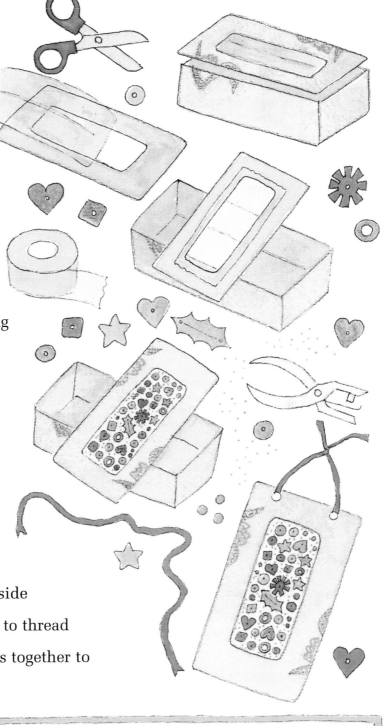

1. Cut around the top of the tissue box to remove it.

2. Carefully pull off the plastic stuck behind the opening of the box.

3. Set the rectangle top, print side down, across the open tissue box so that the opening is not touching any surface. Cover the opening with packing tape.

4. Turn the rectangle over and decorate the sticky tape across the opening with the sequins, craft beads, and glitter.

5. Punch a hole on each end of one side of the rectangle. Cut a piece of ribbon to thread through the two holes and tie the ends together to make a hanger.

Find some rectangle-shaped boxes, such as a spaghetti box, and use them to trace around on a large sheet of construction paper. Overlap the tracings and use lots of different colors to make an interesting rectangle design.

Ms. Square

This puppet friend is a real **square!**

Here is what you need:

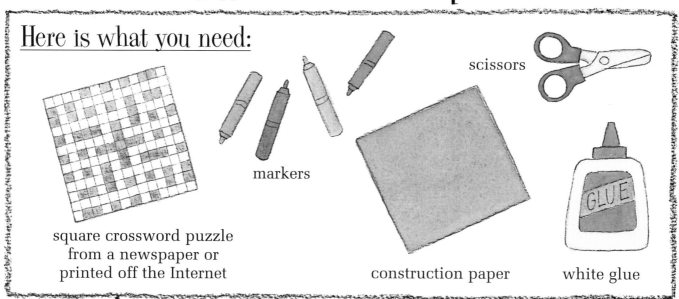

scissors

markers

square crossword puzzle
from a newspaper or
printed off the Internet

construction paper

white glue

Here is what you do:

1. Cut around the square crossword puzzle.

2. Cut two pieces of construction paper the same size as the puzzle.

3. Glue the puzzle to one of the squares of construction paper.

4. Color in some of the squares with markers to give the puzzle a face and some hair.

5. Glue the sides and top of the puzzle to the second square to create a mitt puppet.

Collect crossword puzzles, used or unused, and color in the **squares** to make designs or pictures.

39

Wrapped Square Pin

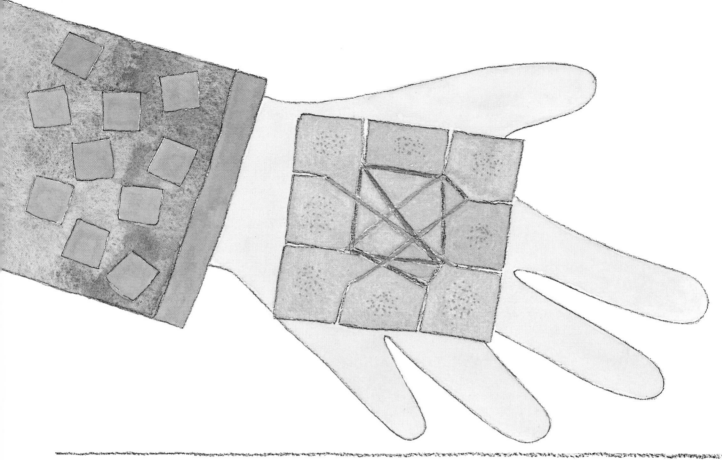

Wear a **square!**

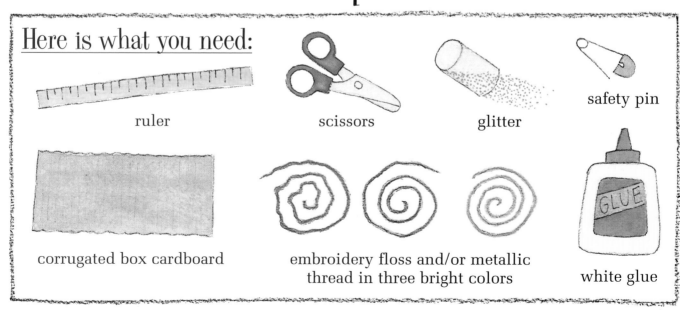

Here is what you need:

ruler

scissors

glitter

safety pin

corrugated box cardboard

embroidery floss and/or metallic thread in three bright colors

white glue

Here is what you do:

1. Cut a 1 3/4-inch (4.5-cm) square from the corrugated box cardboard.

2. Cut 1/4-inch (3/4-cm) slits around the outside of the square.

3. Secure the end of a piece of thread in a slit, gluing the end onto the back of the square. Wrap the square in a crisscross of the thread, securing the other end through a slit and gluing it in back of the square.

4. Do this with at least three different colors of thread.

5. Dab glue between the threads and sprinkle the square pin with glitter.

6. Slip the back of a safety pin through the threads in back of the square.

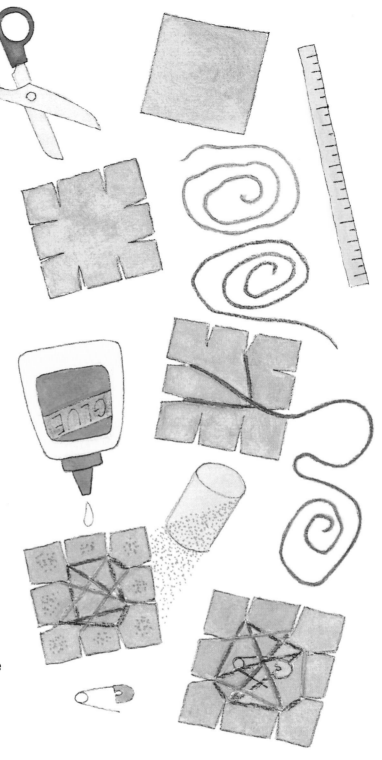

Use an empty **square** box such as jewelry comes in to make a picture of printed **squares**. Just dip the rim of the box in paint and print.

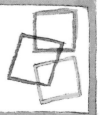

Decorated Post-its™

Make a **square** gift.

Here is what you need:

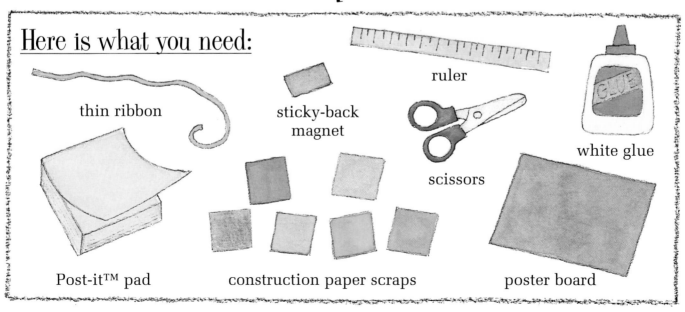

thin ribbon

sticky-back magnet

ruler

scissors

white glue

Post-it™ pad

construction paper scraps

poster board

Here is what you do:

1. Cut a square of poster board that is about 1/4 inch (3/4 cm) bigger than the Post-it™ pad.

2. Glue the pad to the center of the poster board square.

3. Glue a strip of ribbon up the center of the first Post-it™ on the pad. Tie a piece of ribbon in a bow and glue it at the top of the ribbon strip so that the pad looks like a wrapped package.

4. Cut several 1/4-inch (3/4-cm) squares from construction paper scraps. Glue the squares on each side of the ribbon to decorate the paper.

5. Put a piece of sticky-back magnet on the back of the Post-it™ pad. You won't even have to wrap this gift! It is ready to be given to someone special you know.

Use some SQUARE Post-it™ sheets to make a guessing game to play with a friend. Stick three or more Post-its™ in a row on a sheet of construction paper. You might want to number them or color each one a different color to distinguish one from the other. While one person covers his eyes, the other hides a small paper SQUARE under one of the Post-it™ papers. The other person then tries to guess under which Post-it™ the SQUARE is hidden.

Hairy Squarey

Wow! A square with hair!

Here is what you need:

pencil

markers

plastic wrap

pebbles

scissors

soil

grass seed

small pudding box

construction paper scraps

white glue

water

Here is what you do:

1. Cut off the open top and edge of the pudding box to make it exactly square.

2. Trace around the front of the box with the pencil. Cut the square tracing out. Glue the square to the front of the box to cover it.

3. Cut three small squares from the construction paper scraps. Glue them to the front of the box for eyes and a nose. Use the markers to draw a mouth and add details to the square face.

4. Tear off a square of plastic wrap. Push the center down into the box to line it with plastic.

5. Drop some pebbles in the bottom of the box to hold the plastic in place and provide drainage.

6. Fill the box with soil. Sprinkle the soil with grass seed and then water.

7. Place the square in a sunny window and watch it grow some grass "hair."

Paint a net bag and use it to print a page full of tiny **squares**. You might also try printing squares with a plastic berry basket with a bottom made up of smaller squares. What else could you use to print squares?

Shape Snakes

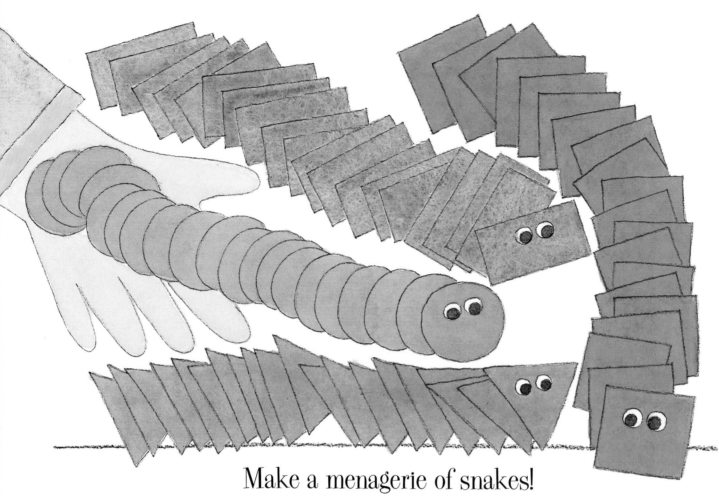

Make a menagerie of snakes!

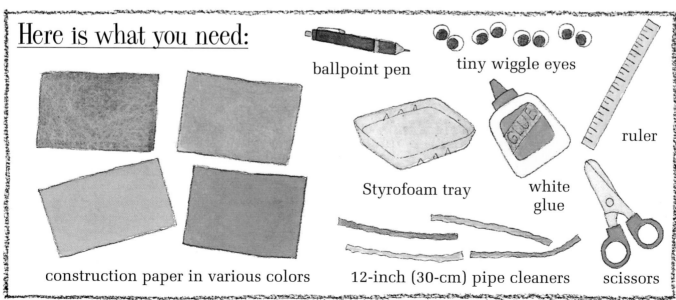

Here is what you need:

ballpoint pen

tiny wiggle eyes

ruler

Styrofoam tray

white glue

construction paper in various colors

12-inch (30-cm) pipe cleaners

scissors

Here is what you do:

1. Decide which shape snake you want to make first. Cut about twenty to twenty-five 2-inch (5-cm) shapes from construction paper.

2. Set each shape on the Styrofoam tray and use the pen to poke a small hole through the center of each one.

3. String the shapes onto the pipe cleaner to make a snake.

4. Glue a shape flat on each end of the pipe cleaner to make the head and the tail of the snake.

5. Glue two wiggle eyes to the head.

6. Make a snake from each of the four shapes in this book.

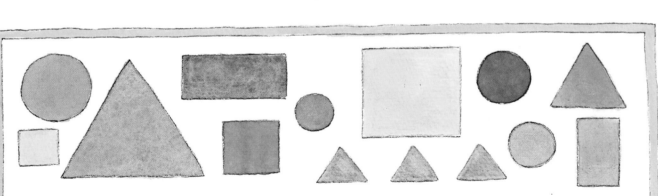

Cut lots of shapes from construction paper in different colors and sizes. Store them in a sturdy box with a lid. Arrange the shapes in the lid of the box to make different shape pictures. You will be amazed at how many things you can make with **circles**, **squares**, **rectangles**, and **triangles**.

About the Author and Artist

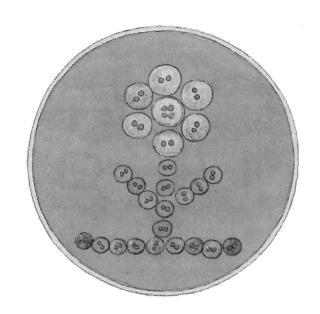

Twenty-five years as a teacher and director of nursery-school programs has given Kathy Ross extensive experience in guiding young children through crafts projects. Among the more than thirty-five craft books she has written are *Crafts for All Seasons, Make Yourself a Monster, Crafts From Your Favorite Fairy Tales, Crafts From Your Favorite Children's Songs, The Best Birthday Parties Ever,* and the *Holiday Crafts for Kids* series.

Jan Barger, originally from Little Rock, Arkansas, now lives in Plumpton, East Sussex, England, with her husband and their cocker spaniel, Tosca. She has written and illustrated a number of children's books and is known for her gentle humor and warm, friendly characters. She also designs greeting cards, sings with the Brighton Festival Chorus, and plays piccolo with the Sinfonia of Arun.

Together, Kathy and Jan have written and illustrated two earlier volumes in this grouping of concept crafts books: *Kathy Ross Crafts Letter Sounds* and *Kathy Ross Crafts Letter Shapes*. They are at work on volumes on colors and numbers.